For:

conversations with
remarkable children™
on friendship

Compiled With the Help of Our Friends

Illustrations by Kerren Barbas

Peter Pauper Press, Inc
White Plains, New York

Book designed by Lesley Ehlers
Illustrations copyright ©1999 Kerren Barbas

Text copyright ©1999
Peter Pauper Press, Inc
202 Mamaroneck Avenue
White Plains, NY 10601
Printed in Singapore
ISBN 088088-900-4
7 6 5 4 3 2 1

The publisher would like to thank
the following for their assistance
in assembling this book:

Black Images Books, Dallas, TX
Books on the Square, Woodstock, IL
The Bookstore, Glen Ellyn, IL
Buchmeister Books, Chatham, NJ
The Children's Center, Patterson, NY
The Davenport Public Library, Davenport, IA
Diana's Bookstore, Elkin, NC
4Kids . . . Of All Ages, Mackinaw City, MI
Hinkle's, Winston-Salem, NC
Learned Owl Bookshop, Hudson, OH
Tudor Book Shop, Kingston, PA

Friends share their toys, give each
other stickers, make stuff together,
do stuff together like sell lemonade.
They listen to each other.
They always like to be together.
They love each other.

Rebecca Joy Briesmoore, age 7

A friend is a person who doesn't lie to you and helps you when you are hurt. They play with you and never talk behind your back. A friend always sticks up for you and never lets you down. Friends always stick together no matter what.

Teresa Marie Spittler, age 10

Friendship is something that never ends and it will always be with you if you're a good friend.

Jane C. Layoff, age 6

Friendship is like playing, having fun,
visiting, and don't fight with him.
Don't try to make the friendship
break apart. I enjoy playing
with my friend, do you?

Erik David Hult, age 6

Friendship is love, sharing,
caring, sadtimes and goodtimes
all bundled up together to have
in your heart forever.

Jamil Clifan Waters, age 8

A real friend is a person who will give anything. It does not matter if it is a boy or a girl, as long as they care.

Alesia Ann Walsh, age 9

Austin is a friend
when I go on his boat.

Coley Darr McCulloch, age 3

Friendship is being with
your friends every day.

Diana Macon McCulloch, age 6

Friends are people you can trust. They help you when you're in trouble. They come on special days, sleep overs, and just to play. If you have a bad friend you just walk away, meet other people and introduce yourself to a newcomer in your neighborhood, school, or around your block.

Amanda P. Dunn, age 9

Friendship is like a big pile of gold. You can use it all and waste it or you can treasure it for ever and ever. When you are an old man or old lady you can look back and see how lucky you were to have such nice friends.

Betsy Erin Thomas, age 9

A good friend should play with you.
I play hide-and-seek with Arianna,
but sometimes she fights with me. I
miss her now that she's in big school.

Caitlin Unser, age 4

A friend helps you out in case you spill something. A friend loves you. They (a friend) would tell your mom if you had something like a broken leg. They help you get better, like a hospital.

McKenzie Kelly, age 5

A friend to me is someone who is nice to you, plays with you, cares about you, and you can trust them. They are there to rub your tired feet or pat your back. My best friend is my mom.

Laura Allison Whitener, age 9

A friend is someone who
would take you for
who you are.

Catharine Linn Bennett, age 10

A friend is someone to do finger-paints in the basement with. Friends are nice. They help me get the bad guys. Friends share their popsicles. A friend is Travis!

Zachary J. Dermont, age 4

A friend helps clean-up. A friend stops and helps a person who is hurt. A friend who cares will help someone who is blind and can't get the phone. A friend helps some people get on a horse. You're excited for a friend when they win $100 in the mail, and happy for them when it's their birthday.

Tina Marie Thompson, age 9

*G*ood friends don't have bad attitudes with you. A good friend isn't selfish or greedy. Most of all a good friend never gets you in trouble for something they cause or they say.

Ayesha Marie Acquah, age 9

Milo is my dog. She is a good friend because she plays with me, licks me, and makes a lot of noise when strangers come.

Jesse Roger Skolnick, age 6

We play twister. When
we're close to each other
we laugh and then fall down.

Ashley Orlando, age 6

A friend is a person who you love,
care about, trust, and a person
who is kind to you.
A friend can never let you down.

Taylor Lee Wright, age 10

A true friend never tells lies
or gives you candy you
don't really want.

Max Malinow, age 9

A friend cares for you and thinks you are wonderful just like you are without changing a thing.

Ashley Rene Allen, age 10

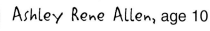

A friend does not boss me.
A friend reads books to me.

Kathleen Whelan O'Meara, age 5

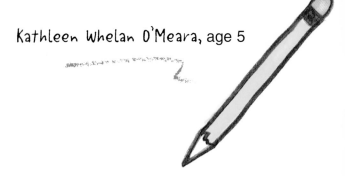

You should help your friends
very much. You should stop the fight
if friends are fighting.

Matthew Paul Spittler, age 5

Friends should sit
next to each other
on the bus.

Connor Craven-Falcón, age 5

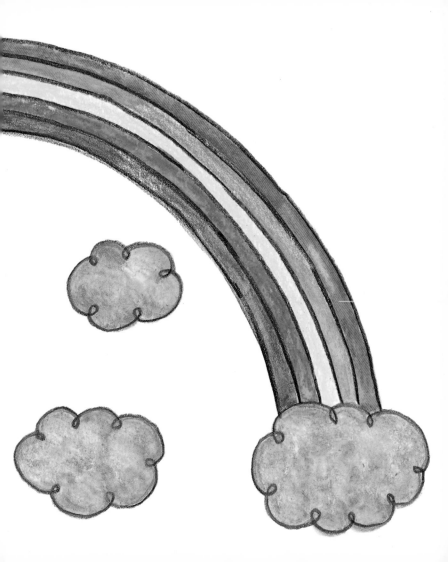

He [a friend] shares his stuff, gets good grades and is smart. Friendship makes you feel safe and relaxed.

Daniel John Hamburg, age 8

You play with her a lot and invite her to your birthday party. A friend dresses pretty and plays nicely. If you don't try to have any friends God won't like you.

Jessica Lee Hamburg, age 6

33

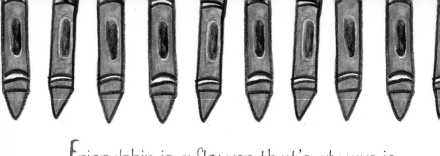

Friendship is a flower that's always in bloom or a piece of music that never stops playing. Friendship is the whole world and all its goodness and love. Finally, friendship gives you something that nothing else can, a friend.

Catherine Armao, age 9

Friends play with you at recess. They help you with things that you can't do, like sports. Hopefully we'll always be friends forever.

Nicholas S. Milton, age 9

Friendship is a great thing
to have in this world.

Jamie Lee Roth, age 8

I always have my cat Dusty with me. I pick him up a lot. He is my friend even though he attacks me.

Meghan P. McKeon, age 6

It's nice to be nice to someone.
Always stick with a friend even
when he is sick or in a bad mood.
Never let him down.

Nicholas W. Krzemienski, age 8

Best friends always look up to each other. When I am in a bad mood my friends try to make me un-grouchy.

Stephanie D'Aquila, age 9

A good friend never tells a friend's private secrets or embarrasses them. Good friends are always willing to help their friend when [the friend] can't do something they can do.

Shantaia R. Griffin, age 9

If my friend tried to go down
the slide backwards, I would
tell her not to. Having the best
toys isn't important. It's just
important to be good friends.

Rebecca Johnson, age 8

Having a friend is better than having a sister sometimes.

Susie Heller, age 4

Friends share stuff with
you. The are funny. Sometimes
they give good jokes.

Sophie Mendelson, age 6

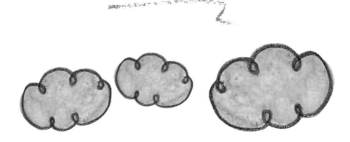

Friendship is very special
to you and me.

Richelle (Lynn) Heiny, age 7

A good friend is someone
who does his or her
homework with me.

Rodney W. Alston, age 10

A friend is a girl or boy in whom you confide and you trust with your inner most secrets. Even if you are not standing by their side, you know they are "with" you in heart and soul. I think if you have a true friend, you are very lucky, for there are not many in this world.

Laura Claire Gilroy, age 9